God the Son

The Lutheran Difference Series

Alfonso Espinosa

Contributions by

Henry Gerike

Edward Engelbrecht

CONCORDIA PUBLISHING HOUSE • SAINT LOUIS

Written by Alfonso Espinosa

Contributions and editing by Henry Gerike and Edward Engelbrecht

Copyright © 2003 by Concordia Publishing House, 3558 S. Jefferson Ave., St. Louis, MO 63118-3968. Manufactured in the U.S.A.

This publication may be available in braille, in large print, or on cassette tape for the visually impaired. Please allow 8 to 12 weeks for delivery. Write to Library for the Blind, 1333 S. Kirkwood Road, St. Louis, MO 63122-7295; call 1-800-433-3954, ext. 1322; or e-mail to blind.library@lcms.org.

All Scripture quotations are from the HOLY BIBLE, NEW INTERNATIONAL VERSION®. NIV®. Copyright © 1973, 1978, 1984 by International Bible Society. Used by permission of Zondervan Publishing House. All rights reserved.

Quotations from the *Concordia Triglotta* are copyright © 1921 by Concordia Publishing House. All rights reserved

All rights reserved. No part of this publication may be reproduced, stored in a retrieval system, or transmitted, in any form or by any means, electronic, mechanical, photocopying, recording, or otherwise, without the prior written permission of Concordia Publishing House.

1 2 3 4 5 6 7 8 9 10   12 11 10 09 08 07 06 05 04 03

Contents

About This Series 4
Student Introduction 5
Overview of Christian Denominations 7
Lutheran Facts 10

Eternal God and Promised Messiah 11
God Became Flesh 15
Sinless Savior 21
Sin-Bearer 26
Risen Savior, Living Lord 30
Head of the Church
          and Coming King 35

Leader Guide Introduction 40
Answers 41
Appendix of Lutheran Teaching 60
Appendix of Christological Controversies 63
Glossary 64

About This Series

"My church is a lot more open-minded than yours."

"What do you mean?"

"Well, we teach that Christians, Jewish people, and Muslims all pray to the same God. You talk as if Jesus were *the* Savior, the only path to God."

As Lutherans interact with other Christians, they often find themselves struggling to explain their beliefs and practices. Although many Lutherans have learned the "what" of the doctrines of the church, they do not always have a full scriptural foundation to share the "why." When confronted with different doctrines, they cannot clearly state their faith, much less understand the differences among denominations.

Because of insecurities about explaining particular doctrines or practices, some Lutherans may avoid opportunities to share what they have learned from Christ and the Scriptures. The Lutheran Difference Bible-study series identifies *how* Lutherans differ from other Christians and demonstrates from the Bible *why* Lutherans differ. These studies can prepare Lutherans to share their faith and to help non-Lutherans understand the Lutheran difference.

Student Introduction

Muslims believe that Jesus was a great prophet. Jewish people believe that Jesus was a gifted yet unorthodox rabbi. Buddhists regard Jesus as an enlightened person. Scholars acclaim Jesus for His remarkable ethics. Jehovah's Witnesses describe Jesus as an exalted, divine being. Mormons teach that Jesus Christ became a god.

But the early *Christ*ians—the people who first followed Jesus Christ, recorded His teachings, and received Baptism in His name—believed that He is God and became a man for the salvation of all who receive Him. They knew Him as God the Son, the Second Person of the Holy Trinity.

Christians today hold the same basic beliefs about who Jesus is and about His work of salvation. The earliest centuries of Christian teaching focused on these beliefs and how Christians should describe them from the Scriptures. Because of human weaknesses and misunderstandings, controversies broke out and even divided the fellowship of the early Christians. (The modern notion that earliest Christianity didn't have denominational differences is false.) Through close adherence to the Scriptures, faithful teaching was maintained. The clarification of doctrine that resulted from these controversies is summarized in the three ecumenical creeds: The Apostles' Creed, The Nicene Creed, and The Athanasian Creed.

Humility and Faith

The controversies that confused and divided the early Christians stemmed from two biblical teachings: (1) Jesus is truly a man and (2) Jesus is truly God. The tension between these truths (paradox) caused various teachers to compromise one of the two truths or to find some way to reconcile them through human logic. (See Christological Controversies, p. 63.)

Much of the controversy stemmed from the confidence of different teachers who thought they could explain the mystery of the human and divine natures in Christ. Although human reason is one of

God's gifts, it is too weak to explain the eternal mysteries of God. In humility, Christian teachers had to learn that they should simply receive and confess what God teaches about Himself in the Scriptures rather than try to satisfy their reason by figuring it all out.

The most important teaching of all is that, for our salvation, Jesus is both truly God and truly man. He paid the price for our sins on the cross and extends that blessing to us today through His Word and Sacraments.

An Overview of Christian Denominations

The following outline of Christian history will help you understand where the different denominations come from and how they are related to one another. Use this outline in connection with the "Comparisons" sections found throughout the study. Statements of belief for the different churches are drawn from their official confessional writings.

The Great Schism

Eastern Orthodox: On July 16, 1054, Cardinal Humbert entered the Cathedral of the Holy Wisdom in Constantinople just before the worship service. He stepped to the altar and left a letter condemning Michael Cerularius, patriarch of Constantinople. Cerularius responded by condemning the letter and its authors. In that moment, Christian churches of the East and West were severed from each other. Their disagreements centered on what bread could be used in the Lord's Supper and the addition of the *Filioque* (Latin for "and the Son") statement to the Nicene Creed.

The Reformation

Lutheran: On June 15, 1520, Pope Leo X wrote a letter condemning Dr. Martin Luther for his Ninety-five Theses. Luther's theses had challenged the sale of indulgences, a fund-raising effort to pay for the building of St. Peter's Cathedral in Rome. The letter charged Luther with heresy and threatened to excommunicate him if he did not retract his writings within 60 days. Luther replied by publicly burning the letter. Leo excommunicated him on January 3, 1521, and condemned all who agreed with Luther or supported his cause.

Reformed: In 1522 the preaching of Ulrich Zwingli in Zurich, Switzerland, convinced people to break their traditional Lenten fast. Also, Zwingli preached that priests should be allowed to marry. When local friars challenged these departures from medieval church practice, the Zurich Council supported Zwingli and agreed that the Bible should guide Christian doctrine and practice. Churches of the Reformed tradition include Presbyterians and Episcopalians.

Anabaptist: In January 1525 Conrad Grebel, a follower of Ulrich Zwingli, rebaptized Georg Blaurock. Blaurock began rebaptizing others and founded the Swiss Brethren. Their insistence on adult believers' Baptism distinguished them from other churches of the Reformation. Anabaptists (*ana* means "again") attracted social extremists who advocated violence in the cause of Christ, complete pacifism, or communal living. Mennonite, Brethren, and Amish churches descend from this movement.

The Counter-Reformation

Roman Catholic: When people call the medieval church "Roman Catholic," they make a common historical mistake. Roman Catholicism as we know it emerged after the Reformation. As early as 1518 Luther and other reformers had appealed to the pope and requested a council to settle the issue of indulgences. Their requests were hindered or denied for a variety of theological and political reasons. Finally, on December 13, 1545, 34 leaders from the churches who opposed the Reformation gathered at the invitation of Pope Paul III. They began the Council of Trent (1545–63), which established the doctrines and practices of Roman Catholicism.

Post-Reformation Movements

Baptist: In 1608 or 1609 John Smyth, a former pastor of the Church of England, baptized himself by pouring water over his head. He formed a congregation of English Separatists in Holland, who opposed the rule of bishops and infant Baptism. This marked the start of the English Baptist churches, which remain divided doctrinally over the theology of John Calvin (Particular Baptists) and Jacob Arminius (General Baptists). In the 1800s the Restoration Movement of Alexander Campbell, a former Presbyterian minister, adopted many Baptist teachings. These churches include the Disciples of Christ (Christian Churches) and the Churches of Christ.

Wesleyan: In 1729 John and Charles Wesley gathered with three other men to study the Scriptures, receive Communion, and discipline one another according to the "method" laid down in the Bible. Later, John Wesley's preaching caused religious revivals in England and America. Methodists, Wesleyans, Nazarenes, and Pentecostals form the Wesleyan family of churches.

Liberal: In 1799 Friedrich Schleiermacher published *Addresses on Religion* in an attempt to make Christianity appealing to people influenced by rationalism. He argued that religion is not a body of doctrines, provable truths, or a system of ethics, but that it belongs to the realm of feelings. His ideas did not lead to the formation of a new denomination, but they deeply influenced Christian thinking. Denominations most thoroughly affected by liberalism are the United Church of Christ, the Disciples of Christ, and Unitarianism.

Lutheran Facts

All who worship the Holy Trinity and trust in Jesus Christ for the forgiveness of sins are regarded by Lutherans as fellow Christians, despite denominational differences.

Lutheran churches first described themselves as *evangelische*, or evangelical, churches. Opponents of these churches called them *Lutheran* after Dr. Martin Luther, the sixteenth-century German church reformer.

Lutherans are not disciples of Dr. Martin Luther but rather are disciples of Jesus Christ. They proudly accept the name *Lutheran* because they agree with Dr. Luther's teaching from the Bible, as summarized in Luther's Small Catechism.

Lutheran teaching centers on Jesus, through whom a person receives the kingdom of God and learns of the heavenly Father. Saving faith is trusting that Jesus Christ died on the cross for the forgiveness of one's sins and rose again from the dead for one's eternal salvation.

Because Jesus is true and eternal God, Lutherans address prayers to Jesus as well as to the Father and the Holy Spirit.

In honor of Jesus, Lutherans stand during the reading of the Gospel in the Divine Service.

A common table prayer used by Lutherans is "Come, Lord Jesus, be our guest. And let Thy gifts to us be blessed." This prayer reminds Lutherans that the daily blessings of God come through Jesus. It also reminds them of Christ's promise to come again on the Last Day.

Lutherans believe that Jesus gives His true body and blood in the Lord's Supper for the forgiveness of sins. This is the chief blessing in the Lord's Supper and is foundational to Lutheran devotion.

To prepare for "Eternal God and Promised Messiah," read John 1:1–18, 40–42a.

Eternal God and Promised Messiah

Infidels now are they who say, "Verily God is the Messiah, Son of Mary."

—The Qur'an 5, 19

Jesus Christ was born around 4 B.C., the child of Mary, a young Jewish woman from Nazareth in Galilee. But He existed before time began! In other words, the Bible teaches the preexistence of Christ. He is truly "the First and the Last" (Revelation 1:17). Jesus is the Savior—the "Messiah" the Israelites knew that God would send. Today, Christians confess that Jesus Christ is the eternal God and promised Messiah!

1. The Bible attributes many names and titles to Jesus Christ, such as "Son of God," "Son of Man," "Messiah," and "Christ." Which titles are most clear and meaningful to you? Which ones are less clear and possibly somewhat confusing?

2. The fact that Jesus is the Messiah was important in the history of the Israelites; the fact that Jesus is God was contrary to the beliefs of most ancient Jews and Gentiles, and it stands in opposition to modern-day beliefs about different paths to "god." Both truths (that Jesus is the Messiah and is God) are vital for knowing Christ. Which one do you think is less understood today? Why?

For All Eternity

3. Read Genesis 1:1. Who existed "in the beginning"? Now read John 1:1, 14. Even while the Word was with God, the Word was _____. According to verse 14, what did the Word become?

4. Read Exodus 3:13–14. What name of God was first revealed to Moses? Read John 8:54–59. What does Christ say of Himself in verse 58? How did the Jewish people who were present at the time react to His words? What was so offensive to them about what Jesus said?

5. Read John 1:40–42a. What does Andrew announce to his brother, Simon Peter? Now look at John 4:25–26. Whom does Christ claim to be in verse 26?

6. Read Daniel 7:13–14. In verse 13, whom did Daniel see (in his vision) approaching the Ancient of Days? How do the people in verse 14 respond to this figure? Read Mark 14:61–64. How did Jesus refer to Himself? Why did the high priest tear his own clothes?

7. Read Psalm 110:1. By inspiration of the Holy Spirit, David records a remarkable conversation. Who is speaking? Whom does the speaker address in this verse? What does God say to King David's Lord? According to Hebrews 1:8, what is the Son—Jesus—called by God the Father? (See Matthew 22:41–46 for further discussion.)

The Appearance of Jesus

You're probably familiar with the saying "Don't judge a book by its cover." In a sense, many people judge Jesus Christ and what He is able to do in terms of His "cover," His appearing as a man.

8. On the basis of what you have learned about Jesus' identity, share what resources Christ makes available to save you and to help you.

9. God's people in the Old Testament waited thousands of years for Messiah (the Christ) to come with His eternal salvation. What does all of this say about the Lord's faithfulness? Since Jesus was faithful to those who waited in Old Testament times for His salvation, what will He do for you as you see clearly that He is the true King of kings?

10. Sometimes Jesus is mixed into the bag of world religions and becomes just another name alongside Buddha, Confucius, Muhammad, the Dalai Lama, and the like. What's wrong with this? What is the major difference between Christ and anyone else whom people might compare Him to?

Jesus Calls You

When you understand the true identity of Jesus Christ, it is amazing to think just how well you can know God.

11. What do you know about God in light of Christ? The list you make may surprise you.

For This Week

Sometimes our prayers are greatly enriched when we approach the Lord through the variety of names and titles given Him in the Bible. Try some of these out as you pray this coming week. Pray to the Lord according to how He is revealed, and "unravel" the meaning of some special names given Him as you pray.

Review hymns such as "All Hail the Power of Jesus' Name" (*LW* 272; *TLH* 339) and "Beautiful Savior" (*LW* 507; *TLH* 657). Note the names/titles given to Jesus. Reflect on how they enrich your worship and your life.

Comparisons

The student introduction presents what different religions say about Jesus of Nazareth. Review this material and note how each group respects Jesus but doesn't understand who Jesus truly is.

Jesus Himself recognized that people held different opinions about Him even before His death and resurrection. When the apostle Peter confidently proclaimed who He was (Matthew 16:13–17), Jesus explained that this faith and understanding was a blessing of the heavenly Father. Faith in Christ does not come from a person's ability to "figure Jesus out." It comes as a gift from God through His Word.

Point to Remember

No one has ever seen God, but God the One and Only, who is at the Father's side, has made Him known. John 1:18

To prepare for "God Became Flesh," read Philippians 2:5–11.

God Became Flesh

Songs of thankfulness and praise, Jesus, Lord, to Thee we raise;
Manifested by the star To the sages from afar,
Branch of royal David's stem In Thy birth at Bethlehem:
Anthems be to Thee addressed, God in flesh made manifest.

Christopher Wordsworth, *LW* 88

It is one thing to know that Jesus Christ is the God who existed before anything was created and the Messiah of Old Testament prophecies, but it is something else to understand that Jesus was still completely God when He took on human flesh. The fact that God became a man is the miracle and the mystery called the Incarnation. (Do not confuse this term with *reincarnation,* a Hindu and Buddhist doctrine—see the glossary p. 64.) The Jesus who walked, slept, spoke, ate, cried, thirsted, taught, became tired, suffered, and died was God on earth.

12. When you consider the depictions of Jesus Christ you've encountered—through art, literature, or the media—is He typically presented as human (like a man) or divine (like God)?

13. At first glance, how might the doctrine of the Incarnation—God taking on human flesh and becoming a man, thereby being both God and man—affect you and your life?

The Birth of Christ

14. Read Isaiah 7:14. What is to come from the virgin? How are these terms related to Jesus' being a man? Which term describes Jesus as being God?

15. Now read Romans 9:5. What does this verse teach us about the human nature of Christ? What is Jesus called in this Bible verse?

16. Did any of this (Jesus' being both man and God) change during Christ's severe humiliation and suffering? Absolutely not! Read 1 Corinthians 2:8. According to this verse, who was crucified?

17. Read Acts 20:28. Whose blood is referred to?

18. Read Colossians 1:15–20. Besides Christ's work of reconciliation on the cross, what other major work of God is attributed to Jesus?

19. Now read Colossians 2:9. How are the divine and human natures of Christ revealed in this verse?

20. Read Philippians 2:5–11. According to verse 6, what is Christ's nature? According to verse 7, what did Jesus will to happen to Himself? The word *appearance* in verse 8 may seem to imply that

Jesus was not really a man. How does the rest of the verse show that Jesus truly was a man? In verses 9–11, who is exalted and worshiped?

It is imperative that we understand the meaning of the biblical description "made Himself nothing." This phrase does not mean that Christ ceased to be God. Consider this insight from Dr. Martin Luther: "He kept it [the majesty of the divine nature] concealed in the state of His humiliation, and did not employ it always, but only when He wished" (The Formula of Concord, Thorough Declaration, Article VIII; *Concordia Triglotta* [St. Louis: Concordia Publishing House, 1921], p. 1,025).

Born for You

21. The Scriptures clearly teach that God was born in time, coming to us in the plainest and clearest way He could have come—as one of us! How might this truth help someone who is searching for God? How does this truth help you as you daily worship God in spirit and truth?

22. The Book of Philippians teaches that Jesus willingly humbled Himself, even to the point of death. What does this say about His love for you? How might this affect the way you live?

Few Christian doctrines are attacked more than the doctrine of Christ's two natures. Many non-Christian cults claim that it is wrong to say Jesus is God. Here are some verses they use against Christian doctrine and the proper interpretation of the Bible:

a. Matthew 24:36—False religions use this Scripture verse to assert that Jesus is not God because Jesus admits to not knowing the day or hour of the end of the world.

b. Matthew 26:39, 42—Cults claim that these verses also prove that Jesus is not God because He is praying *to* God.

c. Colossians 1:15—False religions say that this Scripture verse proves that Christ is not God because it describes Jesus as "the firstborn."

By knowing the biblical teaching on the two natures of Jesus Christ, you can answer these objections to the Christian faith.

23. Equipped with what you have learned about the two natures of Christ, how might you answer the previous three objections to the divinity of Christ?

a.

b.

c.

New Birth for You

The Incarnation and two natures of Christ are doctrines that had to be revealed to us by the Holy Spirit through the Word of God. If these mysteries had never been revealed, no human mind could have conceived the truth about Jesus Christ. Because these doctrines are so contrary to our thoughts and ideas, the church has used the ancient creeds—Apostles', Nicene, and Athanasian—to keep the pure doctrine of God's Word ever before us.

For This Week

Review what the creeds say about the person of Jesus Christ. (Check your hymnal or catechism for the wording of the creeds.)

Thank the Lord that, by virtue of His human nature, He understands and relates to your every need and struggle. While never sinning, He knew hunger, tiredness, tears, thirst, indignation, rejection, hard work, suffering, and even what it means to struggle while in prayer. Then, continue to thank the Lord that, by virtue of His divine nature, He is able to help you and deliver you in your time of need. Even if you must bear a cross, He can and will sustain you. Praise Him that He blesses you so completely because He is both God and man!

Comparisons

The term *creed* comes from the Latin word *credo*, "I believe." Creeds are summary confessions of faith used by the vast majority of Christians. They developed at a time when most people could not read and needed a memorable standard of faith. The root of creeds is in the *shema,* used in ancient Israelite households as part of daily prayer. The *shema* (Hebrew for "hear") is drawn from Deuteronomy 6:4–9, 12–21, and Numbers 15:37–41. It served as a summary of Moses' teaching about God and was probably recited by Jesus and His apostles. (See Mark 12:28–31, where Jesus recites a portion of the *shema* to answer a teacher of the law.)

After Jesus ascended into heaven, the earliest Christians began using summaries of Christian teaching (e.g., see 1 Corinthians 15:3–5). These summaries developed into the first three creeds listed below:

Apostles' Creed. A summary that began to take shape already at the time of the apostles. This creed developed from a series of questions asked of a person at the time of Baptism. History shows that congregations at Rome were using a form of this creed in the second century A.D., but the wording did not receive its standard form until much later. Most churches from the Western (Latin) tradition still use the Apostles' Creed for instruction and as a confession of faith in worship.

Nicene Creed. A summary of Christian teaching adopted by congregations of the Roman Empire at the Council of Nicaea in A.D. 325. The creed was expanded by the Council of Constantinople in 381 to help settle other Christological controversies of the fourth century. Today, Eastern Orthodox churches and most churches from the Western (Latin) tradition confess the Nicene Creed in worship, especially during a Communion service. In the Middle Ages, the Western churches added the *Filioque* statement (see Glossary, p. 64).

Athanasian Creed. A longer creed addressing the Christological controversies of the fourth and fifth centuries A.D. It is named for Athanasius (c. 296–373), a bishop of Alexandria, who vigorously opposed Arianism (see Christological Controversies, p. 63). However, Athanasius did not write this creed, since it emerged much later. Many churches of the Western tradition use the Athanasian Creed. Lutheran congregations typically recite it on Trinity Sunday. The creed has been included in Eastern Orthodox services, minus the *Filioque* statement (see Glossary, p. 64).

No creed but the Bible. Congregations of the Restoration Movement rejected the use of creeds early in the nineteenth century A.D. They taught that creeds divided Christians from one another and that agreement on the Bible as God's Word was a sufficient basis for unity. Christian Churches, the Disciples of Christ, and the Churches of Christ descend from this movement.

Liturgical churches (Eastern Orthodox, Lutheran, Reformed, Roman Catholic, and some Wesleyans) regularly recite a creed during their worship services. Many nonliturgical churches accept the teachings of the creeds but do not use them in their worship services.

Point to Remember

And being found in appearance as a man, He humbled Himself and became obedient to death. Philippians 2:8

To prepare for "Sinless Savior," read Hebrews 4:14–5:10.

Sinless Savior

To what base ends, and by what abject ways,
Are mortals urg'd through sacred lust of praise! . . .
To err is human; to forgive, divine.

Alexander Pope, *An Essay on Criticism: Part 2*

The Bible teaches us that Jesus did not sin. Some people think that because Jesus did not sin He was not fully human, as in the saying "To err is human." At one time, however, Adam and Eve were both fully human and without sin. Through lust of glory, human beings lost their purity.

By placing His sinless life under the Law, Jesus sought to restore our purity. Jesus kept the Law, not for Himself but for us.

24. What is the difference between Jesus' being tempted and your being tempted?

25. Does the fact that Christ was saving us also through His life before His crucifixion and resurrection seem to you to be a well-known teaching in the church? Explain your answer.

One with Us

26. Read Hebrews 4:15. What does this verse say about Jesus' life on earth?

27. Does the fact that Jesus did not sin mean He did not suffer when He was tempted? Read Hebrews 2:18.

28. Read Leviticus 19:1–2. What did the Lord command Moses to reveal about Him? On the basis of your insights gained in the first two sessions, what do these verses say about Jesus Christ?

29. In sinlessness and holiness Jesus came into the world, but there is another important condition to be aware of. Read Galatians 4:4–5. According to verse 4, under what condition was Jesus born? According to verse 5, why was Jesus born in this way?

30. Read Matthew 3:13–15. We need to be baptized because of our sinfulness, but Jesus had no sin. Why was He baptized?

31. Read Matthew 5:17. What did Jesus say He had come to do?

32. Finally, read Romans 10:4. Does the word *end* mean "termination," or does it mean "fulfillment"? (Use the Scripture verse in Question 31 to interpret Scripture.) According to Romans 10:4, what does this truth mean for us?

Essential for Salvation

33. Sometimes people view the sinlessness and holiness of Jesus as a mere expression of piety and respect. But why is Christ's sinlessness and holiness really vital to our being saved?

34. If someone insists that salvation is based on obeying the Law, what does that opinion say about the life, death, and resurrection of Jesus?

35. God looks at you as if you have perfectly kept the Law, because Christ has kept the Law in your place. What response(s) does this teaching stir in you?

36. Because of Christ's sinless life under the Law for us, what kind of attitude can we have toward God's Law in the Bible?

Genuine Love

37. Read 1 Corinthians 13:4–7, inserting your name in place of the words "love" and "it." Reflect. Then read this passage a second time, inserting the name "Jesus" in place of the words "love" and "it." Is there any difference?

For This Week

Use Luther's Small Catechism to help you confess ways you have broken each commandment. Confess how Christ kept the very same commandments for you.

Think of someone you've had difficulty loving. "Wrap" this person in prayer this coming week.

Comparisons

Through the centuries, different teachers have proposed different ideas or emphases about the meaning of Christ's life and death. These are known as theories of the atonement. Here are some important examples:

23

Declaratory view. Christ died to show human beings how much God loves them. Some liberal theologians hold this view today.
Dramatic view. Christ tricked the devil by disguising His divine nature with His human nature. The devil attacked Christ and believed that he overcame Him by means of Christ's cross. But Christ arose from death and defeated the devil. This way of describing Christ's work was popular in early Christianity.
Example view. Christ lived and died as an example of goodness for His followers to imitate. The medieval philosopher Peter Abelard (1079–1142) held this view. A group called the Socinians held this view at the time of the Reformation. Some liberal theologians hold this view today.
Martyr view. Christ gave up His life for a principle of truth in opposition to falsehood. A variation holds that Christ died because of misunderstanding, just as others have died because of human sin and hatred. Some liberal theologians hold this view today.
Satisfaction view. Christ died to satisfy God's perfect justice. Medieval teachers Anselm (1033–1109) and Thomas Aquinas (1225–74) emphasized the satisfaction view. This emphasis has been strong among Roman Catholics.
Substitution view. Christ bore our sins on the cross and received the punishment of death that all people deserved.

Lutherans and other Christian teachers have emphasized *substitutionary satisfaction*, pointing out that the last two views are taught by the Scriptures. Christ both satisfied the Father's justice and substituted His life for ours so that He might reconcile us to God and defeat sin, death, and the devil. Certainly Christ also set a good example for His followers. But following Jesus' example cannot atone for one's own sins.

Point to Remember

We do not have a high priest who is unable to sympathize with our weaknesses, but we have one who has been tempted in every way, just as we are—yet was without sin. Hebrews 4:15

To prepare for "Sin-Bearer," read Romans 3:19–26.

Sin-Bearer

Jesus atoned for the sins of those who accepted his teaching, by being an infallible example to them.

Mahatma Gandhi, *All Men Are Brothers*

Though Jesus truly serves as an example, Christians view His work of atonement as something much greater. They teach that Jesus bore the sins of the world as our sacrifice and substitute.

In sports such as baseball, soccer, and football, one player comes in as a substitute for another. By the end of the game, that substitute may have secured either the victory or defeat for the whole team. The greatest substitution in history was no game, but it was something we share in. Jesus' death on the cross was, in the eyes of God, *our* death. His work of redeeming us is finished, and as a result we are saved.

38. When you see a crucifix, a cross holding a body that depicts Jesus Christ, what do you think of?

39. Some people find Jesus' crucifixion for our sins to be comforting; others find it offensive. Why?

Atonement

Today, people are quick to hold to the truth that God is love. They are not so quick to acknowledge that God has wrath (real and righteous anger that condemns evil).

40. Read Romans 3:25a. What happened to Jesus to turn God's wrath away?

41. Read Romans 5:10. What has caused our being reconciled (restored to friendship) with God?

42. Read Matthew 20:28. What are the two reasons Jesus gives to explain His coming to earth?

"Ransom" refers to the sum of money used to buy back defeated prisoners or slaves. This process is called "redemption." When the Bible says you're "redeemed," it means that you have been delivered from sin and death. Jesus paid the price through His death on the cross to buy you back from sin.

43. Read Hebrews 9:26–28. What did Christ do "once for all"? What did He do with our sins?

44. Read 2 Corinthians 5:21. What words show the method God used to do away with our sins?

"God made Him ... to be sin" does not mean that Jesus became sin *in essence*. He did not become sinful in His being. As He hung on the cross, He was considered, treated, and regarded by God as the sacrifice for all sins. He was viewed and counted as bearing our sins. In truth, God has already and finally dealt with all our sins through the cross of Christ!

45. Read Galatians 3:13. How does Paul describe Jesus' work on the cross? What does this mean?

Your Defense

46. Satan is also known as "the accuser" (see Revelation 12:10). His ongoing practice is to accuse the people of God. He claims that God still holds our sins against us. According to the doctrine of Christ's work, why is the devil's claim absolutely and positively a false accusation, a lie?

47. Based on the preceding overview, is it appropriate for us to say that God has indeed dealt with our sin? Why or why not?

48. Some persons may claim that it's sacrilegious to say that Christ became sin for us. Why would it be sacrilegious to say that He did not?

49. Of the seven recorded sayings of Christ on the cross, perhaps the most perplexing is His crying out to the Father: "My God, My God,

why have You forsaken Me?" (Matthew 27:46). How do the foregoing insights help us explain this?

For This Week

People remain in guilt and shame when they do not know the Gospel, which proclaims that on the cross Jesus took the curse of their sins upon Himself. Do you know anyone carrying around guilt and shame? Consider sharing some of this session's Scripture verses with them.

Look at the hymns under the "Redeemer" and "Justification" (or "Faith and Justification") sections of your hymnal. Find a hymn that teaches what the death and blood of Christ accomplished for us according to the Bible's teaching. Learn this hymn so that the truth of Christ's death for your salvation will be in your heart and mind more and more.

Comparisons

Limited atonement. Reformed churches, which base their teaching on the theology of John Calvin (1509–64), hold that Christ died only for the elect, not for the rest of humanity.
Universal atonement. Lutherans and most other Christians hold that Jesus died for the sins of all people, not just for those of the elect.

Point to Remember

There is no difference, for all have sinned and fall short of the glory of God, and are justified freely by His grace through the redemption that came by Christ Jesus. Romans 3:22b–24

To prepare for "Risen Savior, Living Lord," read 1 Corinthians 15:3–8.

Risen Savior, Living Lord

Seeing is believing.

—a popular proverb

In contrast to this popular saying, Jesus said: "Blessed are those who have not seen and yet have believed" (John 20:29). Or as some have put it, "Believing is seeing."

Our faith, however, is not "blind." Our faith rests on the Scriptures, which record numerous eyewitness accounts of the living Jesus after He rose from the dead. St. Thomas did not touch a ghost; he touched the risen Christ! Since Christ has truly risen from the grave and is alive, our salvation is secure, our faith certain.

50. If Christ had not been raised from death, what would that mean for the Christian faith?

51. Some churches hold that the resurrection of Jesus was only spiritual, not physical. What are your thoughts about this approach to Christ's resurrection?

52. How is Christ's descent into hell connected with His resurrection?

Jesus' Victory

53. Read 1 Peter 3:18–20, a passage about Christ's descent into hell. How do we know that this descent occurred after His death on the cross? What textual clue indicates that Jesus went to hell? What did Jesus do there? While in hell, did He suffer?

54. Read 1 Corinthians 15:3–8. What are the three items "of first importance" mentioned by Paul? How does Paul elaborate on the third item? Why did the risen Christ make so many appearances?

55. Read Matthew 28:1–10. Before appearing to His disciples, to whom did Jesus appear? According to verse nine, what did the women do as they worshiped Jesus?

56. Read Mark 16:14. What did Jesus do first when He appeared to the 11 disciples? How important was the eyewitness testimony of those who saw the living Christ before His disciples did?

57. Read Luke 24:36–43. This is the same event described in Mark 16:14 (Mark gives a summary; Luke records more details). What was the reaction of the disciples toward Jesus? What did Jesus invite them all to do? While the disciples were still in unbelief, what else did Jesus do to show that He was truly risen?

58. Read John 20:24–28. This section shows that the reference to "the Eleven" in Mark 16:14 does not include Thomas (just as the reference to "the Twelve" in John 20:24 does not include Judas Iscariot). After the other disciples tell Thomas about the risen Christ, what is Thomas's reaction to the news? How would you compare Thomas's reaction with the other disciples' reaction to the women's testimony about the resurrection? When Christ appears again a week later, how does He deal with Thomas's unbelief? What is Thomas's response to Christ then?

59. Read about Christ's ascension in Acts 1:9–11. What exciting words are proclaimed to the apostles by the two angels?

Certainty

60. None of us were eyewitnesses of the assassination of President Lincoln, yet we have a great deal of certainty that it was an actual historical event. Why do we have this certainty? Is the eyewitness testimony about the resurrection of Jesus as trustworthy and certain?

61. Many people have recorded evidence concerning Lincoln's assassination. Few, if any, have risked their lives to do so. After Christ rose from the dead, however, the apostles' lives were at stake for preaching the Gospel. What does this say about their certainty that Jesus was alive after being crucified?

62. After they saw Jesus, what else did the disciples do? Why are these actions important to you?

Comfort

63. One of our greatest fears is the fear of death. Think of someone you know who may be struggling with the fear of death. What could you say to them in view of Christ's death and resurrection?

One of the most important characteristics of the early Christians was their belief that Jesus was alive and present with them. Live in the truth that the risen and living Christ is with you wherever you go!

For This Week

Think about all the things we believe in and take for granted because of the eyewitness testimony of others. Grow in boldness for sharing your faith that Christ is risen!

Comparisons

Resurrection of the body. Traditionally, all Christians hold (on the basis of the Scriptures) that Jesus rose from the dead bodily and will reappear bodily at the end of time. He will raise all the dead bodily for the Last Judgment.

Spiritual resurrection. Liberal theologians have been influenced by modern skepticism, which questions the possibility of miracles. As a result, some theologians have proposed "spiritual" views of the resurrection. For example, some of them hold that Jesus didn't really rise from the dead but that He lives on in the hearts of His followers.

Bodily presence in the Lord's Supper. Eastern Orthodox Christians, Lutherans, Roman Catholics, and some others teach that Jesus gives His true body and blood in the Lord's Supper. For example, the Lutheran Confessions state: "By this communicated [divine] power, according to the words of His testament, He can be and truly is present with His body and blood in the Holy Supper, to which He has directed us by His Word; this is possible to no other man, because no man is in such a way united with the divine nature, and installed in such divine almighty majesty and power through and in the personal union of the two natures in Christ, as Jesus, the Son of Mary" (*Concordia Triglotta*, p. 1,025).

Bodily presence in heaven only. The Reformed churches and others hold that Christ's human nature must remain in heaven until the Last Day. Therefore, they conclude that Jesus cannot give His true body and blood in the Lord's Supper. For example, the Westminster Shorter Catechism states that people who receive the Lord's Supper are "not after a corporal and carnal manner, but by faith, made partakers of his body and blood" (Question 96). In other words, the communing is spiritual and not in the body and blood of Christ.

Point to Remember

What I received I passed on to you as of first importance: that Christ died for our sins according to the Scriptures, that He was buried, that He was raised on the third day according to the Scriptures. 1 Corinthians 15:3–4

To prepare for "Head of the Church and Coming King," read Matthew 24:30–31; 25:31–46.

Head of the Church and Coming King

We're more popular than Jesus now. I don't know which will go first—rock 'n' roll or Christianity.

John Lennon

At this moment Jesus Christ is keeping His church, His body of believers, in the saving faith. By His life, death, and resurrection He secured our salvation; but if not for His sustaining and nourishing service right now, we could never be saved. What is more, by virtue of His holding us now in His church, we are prepared to meet Him face-to-face when He comes again in all power and glory!

64. What evidence do you see that Christ is reigning in heaven right now? What benefits are granted to you as a result of His reign?

65. When you hear the words "Jesus is coming soon," what comes to your mind? Why could these words be disconcerting? Why can they be comforting?

Enthroned in Glory

66. Read Ephesians 1:20–22. According to verse 20, where is Christ seated? In verses 21 and 22, how is this seat (position) described? Who benefits from Christ's reign (v. 22)?

67. Read Romans 8:34. Where is Jesus said to be right now? What is Jesus Christ also doing in this position of authority? Who benefits from this activity of Christ?

68. Read Hebrews 9:28. Christ was sacrificed on earth to take away the sins of all people. What will happen when He appears "a second time"? What does this text say that Jesus will bring with Him?

69. Read Matthew 24:30–31. According to verse 30, who will see Christ coming on the clouds of the sky with power and great glory? According to verse 31, what else will our Lord and Savior do when He comes again?

70. Read 1 Thessalonians 4:16–17. In the light of verse 16, what kinds of signs and events will accompany the second coming of Christ? What does the last sentence of verse 17 teach?

71. Read Matthew 25:31–34, 41. According to verse 31, what will Christ do when He comes in His glory? Who will be gathered before Christ, and what will He do to them (v. 32)? According to verses 34 and 41, what will Jesus say to those on His right and those on His left?

72. Read Revelation 7:16–17. Verse 16 describes those in heaven with Christ. What does it say of those who are saved? What does verse 17 teach about Christ? What will God do for us?

Coming with the Clouds

73. Christians comfort fellow believers by saying, "I will pray for you." What comfort comes from knowing that Christ Himself prays for us? Share your thoughts on this assurance from the Bible: God the Son is interceding for you!

A vacation Bible school teacher once took his class of first graders outside to have them peer into the sky as he described the second coming of Christ. When the teacher got to the part about Christ's coming on the clouds, a little girl became scared and hid behind a bush. Adults, too, may be confused and unsure about how they can anticipate the glorious coming of Christ.

74. Why can we Christians be filled with joy as we anticipate the Lord's coming? Why can we be confident that we will be with the Lord, standing among those at Christ's right hand and receiving His comfort in heaven?

In your raised and glorified body, you will enter the new heaven and earth; you will never again suffer; and you will be filled with unspeakable joy. All these things are true because of Christ's love and mercy toward you; they are true because Jesus lived, died, and rose for you.

75. What could you say to Jesus when you enter eternity in your raised and glorified body? How do we live for Jesus in our earthly bodies now?

Fully Prepared

76. Think about the Lord's glorious second coming. How are you preparing for His return? List beliefs and practices that help you.

77. Jesus is coming soon! Do you know any persons who are completely unprepared for His coming to judge all people? Make a list of these people. Begin praying for them today, and ask the Lord to help you witness about Christ to them.

Remember that witnessing does not have to be a painful experience. The best witnesses simply take the initiative to show interest in others. Ask the Lord to lead you in what to say and how to say it. Genuinely enjoy the relationship, and seek opportunities to incorporate the Gospel Word and your faith in Christ as the conversation progresses.

Jesus desires that we have absolute assurance from the comforting descriptions in the Bible about His service for us today and when He comes again. The best way for us to have this confidence is to regularly receive Christ's Word and Sacraments.

For This Week

Evaluate your time in worship and the Bible reading. Make—write out—a regular plan to attend divine services and to read the Bible (even if only for a few minutes a day). Put these plans on your calendar and be prepared to be blessed!

Comparisons

Amillennialism. Eastern Orthodox Christians, Lutherans, Roman Catholics, and some Reformed Christians and Wesleyans hold that Christ rules now through His church. The "thousand years" of Revelation 20 symbolize the present rule of Christ. The Apostles' Creed summarizes the events of the end times from an amillennialist view: Jesus will come to judge the living and the dead, He will resurrect the dead, and the church will enjoy the life everlasting.

Millennialism. Anabaptists, Baptists, and some Reformed Christians and Wesleyans hold that Christ will establish a literal, thousand-year rule on earth. Postmillennialists believe that Christ will return *after* this thousand-year period; premillennialists believe that Christ will return *before* this thousand-year period.

Liberalism. Liberals seek to establish Christ's kingdom on earth through social justice and peace.

Point to Remember

"Then the King will say to those on His right, 'Come, you who are blessed by My Father; take your inheritance, the kingdom prepared for you since the creation of the world.'" Matthew 25:34

Leader Guide

Leaders, please note the different abilities of your class members. Some will easily find the Bible passages listed in this study. Others will struggle. To make participation easier, team up members of the class. For example, if a question asks the class to look up several passages, assign one passage to one group, the second to another, and so on. Divide up the work! Let participants present the different answers they discover.

Each topic is divided into four easy-to-use sections.

Focus introduces key concepts that will be discovered.

Inform guides the participants into the Scriptures to uncover truths concerning a doctrine.

Connect enables participants to apply what is learned in the Bible to their lives and provides them an opportunity to formulate and articulate a defense of a key doctrine.

Vision provides participants with practical suggestions for extending the theme of the lesson out of the classroom and into the world.

Also take note of the "Comparisons" section at the end of each lesson. The editor has drawn this material from the official confessional documents and historical works of the various denominations. The passages describe and compare the denominations so that students can see how Lutherans differ from other Christians and how all Christians share many of the same beliefs and practices. The passages are not polemical.

Eternal God and Promised Messiah

Objectives

By the power of the Holy Spirit working through God's Word, participants will (1) understand that long before His human birth, Jesus Christ existed as the eternal God, (2) worship Christ as the One who fulfills all messianic prophecies in the Old Testament, and (3) possess a greater insight for sharing their confidence that Christ—because of who He is—has all power and authority to save us and provide for our every need.

Opening Worship

Invocation: In the name of the Father and of the Son and of the Holy Spirit. Amen.

Pray: Heavenly Father, we praise You for sending Jesus Christ, Your Only Son, to be our Lord and Savior. We confess that we have failed to call on Him as our God, for whom nothing is impossible. Grant us Your forgiveness, and lead us by the power of the Holy Spirit through Word and Sacrament. Bless us now, that as we study Your Word, You may reveal Christ to us once again. In Jesus' name. Amen.

Focus

Ask for a volunteer to read the introduction.

1. There are many possible responses. Clarify the titles "Son of God," "Son of Man," "Messiah" and "Christ." "Son of God" does *not* mean that Jesus is the *Son* of God as *opposed* to being God Himself. "Son of God" is a divine title. It means that Jesus is of the same *substance* as the Father. (*We* are God's "sons" in the sense of Galatians 3:26—adopted as a result of Christ's saving work for us. So Christ is the Son, as in having the divine nature, but we are "sons" in the sense of being legal heirs of God by His grace through faith in Jesus Christ.)

Jesus often referred to Himself as "Son of Man." In the Aramaic of Jesus' day, this expression meant simply "a person." However, the prophet Daniel had used a similar expression to describe the Messiah (Daniel 7:13–14). Therefore, Jesus also used this as a divine title, associated with His authority to save and judge all people (Matthew 20:28; Matthew 25:31).

"Christ" is the Greek equivalent of the Hebrew "Messiah." In Matthew 16:16, Peter identifies Jesus as the Christ—that is, the Anointed One, the long-awaited Messiah who would save His people.

2. Discuss whether people understand the title "Messiah." Also discuss the fact that it is always appropriate to say, "Jesus is God." The Bible clearly teaches this truth (John 20:28; 1 John 5:20).

For All Eternity (Inform)

3. Genesis 1:1—*God* existed "in the beginning." As stated in John 1:1, not only was the Word (Jesus) *with* God; the Word *was* God. John 1:14 teaches that God the Word became flesh (Jesus was conceived and born). These verses reveal the preexistence of Christ by clearly identifying Christ as the Word who is God. Even before space and time began, the Word—our King and Lord Jesus Christ—existed.

4. God reveals to Moses that His name is "I AM"—or *Yahweh* (represented as LORD in English translations). This name of God teaches that He causes all things to come into existence; He has all power and authority. John 8:58 records that Christ attributed this name to Himself. Abraham lived approximately 2,000 years before Jesus was born; nevertheless, as the great "I AM" Jesus existed before Abraham! The Jews who were present reacted as they did because "a mere man" was claiming to be God, a blasphemous claim in their minds and worthy of the death penalty.

5. St. Andrew's announcement was "We have found the Messiah [the Christ]" (John 1:41). As a good Israelite, Andrew had been waiting for the coming Anointed One promised in the Old Testament. He recognized Jesus as the Messiah. In John 4:25–26 the Samaritan woman—a descendant of the tribes in the Northern Kingdom of Israel—also knew the prophecies about the Messiah. Jesus told her, "I who speak to you am He." God brought His Old Testament prophecies to fulfillment in the Lord Jesus Christ.

6. Over 500 years before Jesus's birth, God revealed several messianic prophecies through Daniel (Daniel 7:13–14). Daniel saw "one like a son of man" approaching the "Ancient of Days" (God). This "son of man" was "given authority, glory and sovereign power [and] all peoples, nations and men of every language worshiped Him." In Mark 14:61–64, Christ is being interrogated before the Jewish Sanhedrin. The high priest asked, "Are You the Christ [Messiah], the Son of the Blessed One [and therefore divine]?" "I am," said Jesus. Then He cited Daniel 7. Jesus testifies that He is the Messiah prophesied by Daniel. The high priest tore his clothes in response, and he accused Christ of blasphemy. He understood *exactly* what Jesus had said and determined to kill Him.

7. In Psalm 110:1 the Lord (the heavenly Father) speaks to the Lord (the Son of God), King David's Messiah. God is speaking to God! The proclamation is: "Sit at My right hand until I make Your enemies a footstool for Your feet." Note the reference to "right hand." The Father gives the Son all power and authority. King David lived approximately 1,000 years before Jesus was born, yet he already knew Christ as his Lord and King! Hebrews 1:8 clearly presents the Father as calling the Son "God"!

The Appearance of Jesus (Connect)

8. Jesus can do anything for us, because He is almighty God! Nothing is too hard for Him; nothing is impossible for Him! He can and does meet our every need. All resources are at His disposal because all things belong to Him. If we have Christ, we have the answer to all our needs (Luke 10:41–42).

9. Second Peter 3:9 teaches us that the Lord is not slow in keeping His promises and is patient so that people may come to repentance. He is faithful! The messianic prophecies fulfilled in Christ are proof of that! When we wait for the Lord, we will be blessed (Isaiah 30:18).

10. All other religious leaders in the history of humankind were mere people created by God. Jesus Christ *is* God.

Jesus Calls You (Vision)

11. Answers will vary.

God Became Flesh

Objectives

By the power of the Holy Spirit working through God's Word, participants will (1) confess that God took on human flesh in Christ so that through Him, all of us with human flesh would be saved; (2) worship Christ as the Creator and as the Savior who understands us and relates to us as a brother; and (3) understand how and why the Bible presents Jesus as our all-powerful God and as One who knows the limitations of a human being.

Opening Worship

Invocation: In the name of the Father and of the Son and of the Holy Spirit. Amen.

Pray: Gracious heavenly Father, thank You for sending Christ, Your Son and our eternal God, to be born in time as we are born. We confess that on account of our sinfulness we forget the benefits of the wonderful truth that God became flesh. Grant us Your forgiveness, and lead us once again through Word and Sacrament to confess Christ as true God and true man. Bless us as we study Your Word today. In Jesus' name. Amen.

Focus

Ask for a volunteer to read aloud the introductory paragraph. Point out that throughout history the doctrine that Christ is true God has been under attack. In the fourth century A.D., a false teacher named Arius asserted that Christ had to be a created being. He thus denied the true divinity of Christ. The ancient church responded through the Nicene Creed, stating that Jesus Christ is "begotten, not made, being of one substance with the Father." Unfortunately, various forms of Arianism are alive and well today (e.g., Jehovah's Witnesses). The body of Christ must always be prepared to "test the spirits" (1 John 4:1) through the powerful Word of God.

12. Though the Word of God reveals Christ as fully God and fully man, popular depictions have a tendency to be one-sided. However, many artistic works bring out the biblical revelation that Jesus is both God and man. (E.g., "Adoration of the Magi" by Da Vinci and Fabriano's work of the same title portray the Magi worshiping the Christ Child; both the humanity and divinity of Christ are thus presented.)

13. Jesus is both God and man; that fact is vital to our lives. Some people may be tempted to treat this doctrine as nit-picking and not really important, but nothing could be further from the truth. If Christ were *not* what the Scriptures reveal Him to be, He could not be our Savior.

The Birth of Christ (Inform)

14. This verse describes what comes from the virgin as "child," "son," and "Immanuel." The first two terms point to Christ's human nature. The third points to Christ's divinity ("Immanuel" means "God with us").

Optional: Have volunteers read the quotations from The Augsburg Confession and the Thorough Declaration VIII.24 (appendix p. 62). "Mother of God" is a title for Mary from the ancient Christian church. The virgin gave birth to "Immanuel," God with us.

15. This verse describes Jesus' human nature in terms of His "human ancestry." The answer to the second question is that Jesus is called God! It is a false claim and myth that Jesus is not actually called "God" in the Bible. He is! See also the Thorough Declaration VIII.6 (p. 62). This will reinforce the teaching about the two natures of Christ.

16. Christ's true divinity and humanity did *not* change one iota during His suffering and crucifixion. Read 1 Corinthians 2:8. This verse clearly states that the One put on the cross is "the Lord of glory." This is yet another title of divinity for Jesus.

17. Ask for a volunteer to read Acts 20:28. *God's* blood is referred to. Some English Bibles note the fact that some Greek manuscripts refer to the "Lord's" blood. Another group of Greek manuscripts have the two words side by side ("Lord and God's"). The

blood referred to is from the Lord, who is God. Thus the blood is indeed God's blood.

Read the Thorough Declaration VIII.40, 42, 44 (appendix p. 62). Whoever understands the scriptural revelation that the one person Jesus is truly God and man will understand why "God died" is a biblical and accurate statement.

18. The other major work attributed to Jesus Christ is that of creation! Jesus created all things!

19. Christ's divine nature is described via the words "all the fullness of the Deity." Christ's human nature is described by the words "in bodily form." To be God is to be fully divine. To be human is to have a body. Jesus was fully divine *and* had a body.

20. Verse 6 states that Christ's *being* is by very nature "God" (divine). Verse 7 states that Jesus "made Himself nothing." This means that He "emptied Himself." Verse 8 states that Jesus actually experienced death: thus He was truly a human being. His "appearance as a man" means that He came into the world as an actual man even while He was always God at the same time. Verses 9–11 describe the exaltation and worship of Christ. The Bible never attributes this kind of glory and honor to anyone other than *God Himself!*

Born for You (Connect)

21. One of the saddest and most unfortunate facets of religion is that some people think they must embark on searches and journeys for God. However, the Bible clearly teaches that God embarked on a "journey" for us. He found us! He came into our flesh and joined us in our life. This has not changed at all for the Christian church; to this day Christ continues to come to us through His Word and Sacraments. But God does call us to "seek" Him while He may be found (Isaiah 55:6). He is found through Jesus Christ. Share your thoughts and answers.

22. It is easy to forget that all the humiliation, the "emptying," of Christ was totally and completely based on the free and willful choice of Christ Himself. He willed to make Himself nothing; He chose to empty Himself. Share your thoughts and responses.

23. The false teacher named Arius lived in the fourth century A.D., yet Arianism (see "Christological Controversies," p. 63) is alive and well today. This is especially true in many non-Christian cults, some of which delight in calling themselves "Christian." What follows

are some of their favorite biblical references used to argue against Christ's being God. Call attention to the fact that in every case an answer can be given from the doctrine of Christ's two natures.

    a. Matthew 24:36 contains an example of what Philippians 2:5–7 states: "Christ Jesus . . ., being in very nature God, . . . made Himself nothing." He chose to limit His knowledge in His state of humiliation. However, this does not cancel the fact that He was still God. As God, He knew all things; but this ability He willfully and genuinely laid aside for a time.

    b. Cults ask: "If Jesus is God, why is He praying *to* God?" However, they exclude the biblical doctrine of Christ's two natures. Because He humbled Himself while on earth, Jesus genuinely needed the heavenly Father. He chose to relate to His Father as a weak and humble man so that He could be the Savior of us all.

    c. Cults also use Colossians 1:15 to contradict the true, Christian faith. They argue that if Jesus is "the firstborn," He cannot be God because God is not "born." Ironically, the title "firstborn" means the opposite of what false teachers claim. It is a *title of position,* not substance. (For example, Psalm 89:27 indicates that God appointed David as His "firstborn" when He made him king. David was not "firstborn" in a literal sense—see 1 Samuel 16:10–13.) "Firstborn" describes Christ's position of authority as Lord and God. The very next verse (Colossians 1:16) goes on to teach that Christ created all things! According to His human nature He *was* born, but this in no way contradicts His divine status as "the firstborn over all creation"!

New Birth for You (Vision)

    Conclude by reading the paragraph about the mysteries summarized in the three ancient creeds.

Sinless Savior

Objectives

By the power of the Holy Spirit working through God's Word, participants will (1) understand that Christ could not sin even though He was truly tempted, (2) worship Christ as the One who kept the Law perfectly in our stead, and (3) share the comforting message that Christ kept the Law for the salvation of all people.

Opening Worship

Invocation: In the name of the Father and of the Son and of the Holy Spirit. Amen.

Sing "How Sweet the Name of Jesus Sounds" (*LW* 279).

Focus

Read the introductory paragraph. As we delve into the importance of Christ's keeping the Law for us, we should understand that His sinlessness in no way disqualified Him from truly representing us.

The saying "To err is human" is in a sense a serious misnomer, because sin is a perversion of God's creation. Not only were Adam and Eve fully human before the Fall, but Christians in heaven are also fully human (e.g., they do not "become" angels). What is more, after we rise from the dead, we will still be fully human—even as Christ is still fully human though also fully God. The point is, we often forget that sin is an inherited and spiritual disease that does not make us *more* human. We would never say to anyone that they have to have a particular illness or injury to be fully human. Christ took on flesh and became our brother in the sense that He completely joined us in our humanity. Being born under the Law, He was truly our representative and was in the perfect position—as true God and man—to live for us in a vicarious fashion (as our substitute). Being sinless did not disqualify Him from living for us. It was the reason His living for us under the Law made Him our Savior. He was able to keep the Law perfectly (without sinning) for us all!

24. Share thoughts, but be sure to conclude with the fundamental difference: we are tempted, we may sin; but Christ never sinned when He was tempted. We cannot fathom what this is like, but from God's Word we know it is true.

25. The life of Christ is often treated as if His only purpose were to teach and/or perform the miracles that authenticated His teaching. Many people leave out the fact that He was living *for us* under the Law.

One with Us (Inform)

26. Christ was "tempted in every way, just as we are—yet was without sin." A good example of our Lord's being confronted with diverse temptations is the series of episodes in the wilderness (Matthew 4, Mark 1, and Luke 4).

27. Hebrews 2:18 proves that Christ's temptations were completely real and caused Him to suffer.

28. Leviticus 19:1–2 confirms that Jesus was and is and ever will be holy because He is God. Also, after His incarnation He was holy—completely separate from sin.

29. Galatians 4:4–5 teaches that Jesus was also "born under law." That is, He subjected Himself to God's Law as given to Moses and to His holy nation, Israel. Even though Jesus as God gave the Law, He put Himself under it and put Himself in the position to keep it.

Verse 5 clearly shows Jesus' purpose for being "born under law." It was "to redeem those under law, that we might receive the full rights of sons." Jesus' purpose for putting Himself under the Law was to save us.

30. Matthew 3:13–15 records that Jesus was baptized "to fulfill all righteousness." Through His baptism Christ completely identified with us and showed Himself to be our vicarious (substitutionary) representative. He was already perfectly righteous, but He would fulfill all righteousness for all of us, the unrighteous. Jesus was baptized for us, not for Himself!

31. Jesus did "not come to abolish [the Law or the Prophets] but to fulfill them." He fulfilled all the messianic prophecies, thereby

giving full meaning to the Law and the Prophets, which pointed forward to Him. He also fulfilled all that the Law and the Prophets required of God's people.

32. "End" here does not mean "termination" but "fulfillment." God's Law is good and holy, and we are to cherish it. But Christ is "the end of the law" in that He fulfilled all its righteous requirements for us. Thus, as God's people we are no longer "under the law" but are free from its condemnation. God declares us righteous as we believe in His Son, who fulfilled the Law in our stead.

Essential for Salvation (Connect)

33. If Christ were not the sinless Son of God, He could never have been in the position to fulfill the Law in our stead. If He had been anything else, we would still be under the Law and its condemnation.

34. Such an opinion says that Christ's life was not necessary! Romans 3:20 proves that we cannot make ourselves righteous by observing the Law. Apart from Christ, the Law can only show us our sin—it condemns us. We cannot fulfill the Law; we need Christ to do this for us. And He did!

35. Share responses.

36. We relate to the words in Psalm 112:1—"Praise the LORD. Blessed is the man who fears the LORD, who finds great delight in His commands." God's Law is no longer burdensome, because Christ took away the burden in fulfilling the Law. In Christ, the Law does not condemn us; rather, it shows us the life that Christ lived for us and the life we delight to live.

Genuine Love (Vision)

37. Invite participants to share their insights.

Sin-Bearer

Objectives

By the power of the Holy Spirit working through God's Word, participants will (1) confess the significance of Jesus' shedding His blood on the cross; (2) worship Christ, who was our literal substitute on the cross, so that the wrath intended for us was put upon Him; and (3) share what Christ's death on the cross means—that beyond any doubt, God loves all people and views them as forgiven.

Opening Worship

Invocation: In the name of the Father and of the Son and of the Holy Spirit. Amen.

Sing "Jesus, Your Blood and Righteousness" (*LW* 362).

Focus

Ask a volunteer to read aloud the introduction.

Romans 6:3 teaches that we "were baptized into His death." In Christ's death, our death died. That is, His death was the result of *our* condemnation for sin. In this sense, Christ's death was our death. For the Christian, temporal death is now much more than a consequence of sin entering the world; it is also a blessing. St. Paul says, "To me, to live is Christ and to die is gain" (Philippians 1:21). Death is destroyed and no longer threatens the Christian on account of Christ's substitutionary death.

38. Consider 1 Corinthians 2:2—"I resolved to know nothing while I was with you except Jesus Christ and Him crucified." The cross is not a mere *symbol* of God's love or just an *example* of sacrificial living and dying. St. Paul knew that the cross of Christ is the basis for our salvation—it was where Jesus took away our sins!

39. Consider 1 Corinthians 1:18—"The message of the cross is foolishness to those who are perishing, but to us who are being saved it is the power of God."

Atonement (Inform)

40. Jesus was presented or displayed as "a sacrifice of atonement." Another translation is "propitiation," which can mean "a turning away of wrath." Thus, Christ was sacrificed for us to turn God's wrath away from us.

Read Apology III.261 (appendix p. 60).

Another way of understanding the effect of propitiation is that "our sins have been blotted out by the death of Christ." God's wrath has nowhere else to go because it was put fully upon Christ. In effect, therefore, sins paid for are no more. They're gone—"blotted out."

41. Romans 5:10 clearly teaches that "we were reconciled to Him through the death of His Son." Because of our sins, we were enemies of God; but now that Christ has removed our sins, we are God's friends. We have been reunited with Him, brought back together in harmony, and restored to friendship.

42. Christ came *to serve* and *to give His life* as a ransom for many. "Many" does not mean that the benefits of His death are limited to a special few. For example, 1 John 2:2 says: "He is the atoning sacrifice for our sins, and not only for ours but also for the sins of the whole world."

Note: If the question comes up "To whom did Christ pay the ransom?" Reply that He paid it to the Father, not to the devil!

43. Christ sacrificed/offered Himself once for all (Hebrews 9:26). As a result, Christ was able to "do away with sin" (v. 26) and "take away the sins of many people" (v. 28).

44. Jesus "became sin" because our sin was imputed to Him; we become holy because Christ's righteousness was imputed to us. We are now holy, not by nature but because God declares us holy. On the cross Jesus was declared a sinner, but He was not by nature a sinner.

45. Christ could never be counted as sin in what He did, because He was sinless and always kept the Law of God. However, Galatians 3:13 quotes Deuteronomy 21:23, which teaches that anyone who is hung on a tree is under God's curse. Christ allowed Himself to be hung on a tree so as to be a real and actual substitute for sinners. We are

cursed for what we've done; He was cursed for what He allowed to be done to Him. In this way, a cursed one—one who "became sin"—could die for sinners, for cursed people. It would be hard to find a better commentary on Galatians than Luther's 1531 lectures (published in 1535). Luther depicts the Father as sending His Son to go from heaven to earth to be the worst sinner by taking the sins of all people. The fact that Jesus became a curse for us is the sweetest medicine against a conscience plagued by sin. Our curse is gone. Christ removed it!

Your Defense (Connect)

46. Satan's accusations are an absolute lie because our guilt and shame were put on Christ when He died on the cross. There He cried, "It is finished!"

47. God has indeed dealt with our sin, because Christ was our substitute—"sin for us." As true God and true man, He accepted the punishment, suffering, and death due each of us on account of our sins.

48. We must say what the Bible clearly teaches. The Gospel cannot be understood apart from the truth that Christ became sin for us.

49. Jesus cried out because, by taking our place, He was being treated as we deserved to be treated. On our behalf Christ bore the agony of God's wrath against our sins. As the Father turned away from our sins, He turned away from His Son, who was bearing those sins.

For This Week (Vision)

Urge participants to complete one or both of the suggested activities during the coming week. If time permits, discuss the activities.

Risen Savior, Living Lord

Objectives

By the power of the Holy Spirit working through God's Word, participants will (1) understand why Scripture places so much emphasis on the eyewitness accounts of Christ's resurrection, (2) worship Christ as the One who bodily rose from the grave, and (3) share the truth that our salvation is guaranteed by Christ's resurrection.

Opening Worship

Invocation: In the name of the Father and of the Son and of the Holy Spirit. Amen.

Sing "I Know that My Redeemer Lives" (*LW* 264).

Focus

Ask a volunteer to read aloud the introduction.

Faith is not contrary to reason. Remember the great command to love the Lord our God with all our heart, soul, and mind (Matthew 22:37). We do not practice *fideism*—that is, having faith in faith itself. We do not believe in faith; we believe in Christ! Our faith is therefore intelligent, logical, and rational. God does not call us to blind faith. Jesus Himself led people to believe in Him on the evidence of the miracles He did (John 14:11). Our faith involves real events, people, and places. The historical fact of Jesus' resurrection is the supreme testimony to the truthfulness of the Gospel!

50. 1 Corinthians 15:14 states: "If Christ has not been raised, our preaching is useless and so is your faith." Furthermore, St. Paul declares: "If Christ has not been raised, your faith is futile; you are still in your sins" (1 Corinthians 15:17). Jesus' resurrection is indispensable. If Christ did not rise, there *is* no Christian faith. "But Christ has indeed been raised from the dead" (1 Corinthians 15:20).

51. Christ's resurrection was bodily and physical. His body was dead; it became alive. Liberal critics hold to the rationalistic assumption that miracles are impossible. Logically speaking, if God exists He can work miracles. History testifies to this fact.

52. Encourage people to share their thoughts, but point out that there is some confusion regarding Christ's descent into hell. For now, assure everyone that Christ's descent into hell was not for the purpose of suffering; rather, it was a stage of His glorious resurrection from the dead.

Jesus' Victory (Inform)

53. Christ's descent happened after His death on the cross because the text says in verse 18b: "He was put to death in the body but made alive by the Spirit." The textual clue that Jesus went to hell is twofold: (1) "spirits in prison" and (2) "who disobeyed long ago." The Bible clearly teaches that after people die, their spirit enters either heaven or hell (Luke 23:43; 16:22–23).

"Prison" refers to hell, which is described in terms of agony and suffering. Believers who enter eternal life have had their sins removed by Christ. Their sins are no longer remembered (Isaiah 43:25). The spirits mentioned in 1 Peter 3 disobeyed in Noah's day. They are not in heaven but in hell. Jesus went to "preach" there. Nothing indicates that He suffered. The idea that He would suffer after His death on the cross contradicts the very words of Christ from the cross: "It is finished" (John 19:30; see also Ephesians 4:7–10).

54. The three elements of "first importance" are (1) Christ died for our sins; (2) He was buried; and (3) He was raised on the third day. The third element—the resurrection—is elaborated upon by an extensive list of Christ's many appearances, including one to over 500 followers. Discuss the last question. The Lord was providing ample eyewitness testimony! At the time of Paul's recording of the witnesses, he was effectively inviting any skeptics to check out the facts for themselves!

55. Jesus appeared to the women who had gone early to His tomb (see also Mark 16:1 and Luke 24:10 for the list of women). Verse nine indicates that the women "clasped His feet" when they worshiped Jesus. These kinds of details provide further evidence of Christ's physical, bodily resurrection.

56. He rebuked them "for their lack of faith and their stubborn refusal to believe those who had seen Him after He had risen." Jesus made eyewitness testimony a high priority.

57. The disciples "were startled and frightened, thinking they saw a ghost" (v. 37). Jesus invited them to touch Him and see His real flesh (v. 39). He then asked for something to eat (vv. 41–43).

58. Thomas reacted as the other disciples had done—with doubt and unbelief. Jesus offered the evidence of His physical body and invited Thomas to touch Him. Thomas's response proves that the Bible identifies Jesus as God.

59. The angels proclaim: "This same Jesus, who has been taken from you into heaven, will come back in the same way you have seen Him go into heaven" (v. 11b). Jesus Christ—true God and true man—is risen, has ascended into heaven, and will come again!

Certainty (Connect)

60. Everyone acknowledges the integrity and usefulness of legitimate eyewitness testimony. None of us doubt the existence of Plato or Aristotle. We are certain of Alexander the Great's conquests. We know that John Adams was the second president of the United States. The quality of the eyewitness testimony concerning the resurrection of Jesus Christ is just as good if not better than that concerning the examples mentioned here.

61. What makes the eyewitness testimony about Christ's resurrection so outstanding is that the disciples were willing to give their very lives as they went about their witnessing. People will sometimes go to great lengths to tell a lie, but they will rarely die for a lie. The apostles were dying for the truth of the resurrection!

62. The disciples touched the Lord, clasped Him, and ate with Him (see John 21:12–14). These additional elements are important because they give us proof that Christ truly rose from the dead.

Comfort (Vision)

63. Participants could comfort people with the knowledge that because Christ rose from the dead, we too shall rise.

Head of the Church and Coming King

Objectives

By the power of the Holy Spirit working through God's Word, participants will (1) understand that our salvation/eternal life is entirely sustained through the reign and intercession of Jesus Christ; (2) worship Christ as the One who keeps us in His church and who will welcome us into heaven; and (3) possess a greater urgency for witnessing, since Christ is coming soon to judge all people.

Opening Worship

Invocation: In the name of the Father and of the Son and of the Holy Spirit. Amen.

Sing "Crown Him with Many Crowns" (*LW* 278).

Focus

Ask for a volunteer to read aloud the introduction.

64. Jesus sustains the creation and the governments of the world. In His body, the church, He sustains us through His Word and Sacraments and keeps us in the forgiveness of sins and the assurance of life eternal. In the kingdom of glory we will experience the fulfillment of all His promises, when we will see our Savior face-to-face.

65. How people react to these words depends much on their knowledge of God's Word and on their spiritual condition. To take comfort in the forgiveness of sins through Christ is also to take comfort in His second coming, because He will welcome into the new heaven and earth those who trust in Him. On the other hand, if people do not know that their sins are forgiven, the prospect of Christ's coming may be at least disturbing and at worst a terrifying nightmare.

Enthroned in Glory (Inform)

66. According to Ephesians 1:20, Christ is seated at the right hand of God in the heavenly realms. "The right hand of God" is not a local or circumscribed place. Jesus is not limited to a geographical point on a heavenly map. "The right hand" is Christ's position of power and authority. Verses 21 and 22 describe this position as being "far above all rule and authority, power and dominion, and every title that can be given, not only in the present age but also in the one to come," adding that "God placed all things under His feet and appointed Him to be head over everything for the church." The beneficiaries of this rule and authority of Christ are those in "the church."

67. Again, Jesus is said to be "at the right hand of God" (Romans 8:34). Christ reigns with all power and authority right now. In this position Jesus is "also interceding for us." We are the beneficiaries of His prayers to the Father on our behalf.

68. Hebrews 9:28 teaches that Christ "will appear a second time." In this context, His first-time appearance refers to His incarnation and birth. The second appearance refers to His glorious second coming. Christ will "bring salvation to those who are waiting for Him." This in no way contradicts the fact that we have salvation in Christ today. We do; but throughout the Scriptures our salvation is described as something accomplished, something we are constantly given, and something that is yet to come. These are not contradictory but complementary. The salvation we have now will be confirmed and will lead to a glorious reward in the future.

69. Matthew 24:30 records that "all the nations of the earth" will see the second, glorious coming of Christ. The next verse indicates that Christ "will send His angels with a loud trumpet call" to gather the elect, all Christians. When Christ comes again, He will direct all the events on the Last Day.

70. First Thessalonians 4:16 lists other signs and events that will accompany Christ's glorious coming. There will be (1) "a loud command," (2) "the voice of the archangel," and (3) "the trumpet call of God." Also, (4) "the dead in Christ will rise first." Verse 17 concludes: "We will be with the Lord forever."

71. According to Matthew 25:31, Christ "will sit on His throne in heavenly glory" when He comes again. In verse 32, Jesus teaches us that He will separate people from all nations "as a shepherd separates

the sheep from the goats." This describes the great universal judgment. Verse 34 records that to the sheep Christ will speak words that are sweet: "Come, you who are blessed by My Father; take your inheritance, the kingdom prepared for you since the creation of the world." However, verse 41 records words of terrible judgment spoken to those who rejected Christ: "Depart from Me, you who are cursed, into the eternal fire prepared for the devil and his angels."

Note that Romans 8:1 says: "There is now no condemnation for those who are in Christ Jesus." Galatians 3:13 clearly presents that Christ became a curse for us. But what happens when someone is not "in Christ Jesus"? What happens when anyone rejects Christ's work of becoming a curse for all people? Answer: Their curse remains. To be sure, John 3:16; 2 Corinthians 5:15; 1 John 2:2; and other Scriptures clearly teach that Christ died for the sins *of the world.* But some people never come to saving faith in the glorious work of Christ. When Christians are judged, they are judged in Christ and covered by Him; but when those without Christ are judged, their sins remain without the covering of Christ, whom they rejected.

72. Revelation 7:16 describes those saved by Christ as never again knowing hunger or thirst; the suffering associated with this temporal realm will be gone. Verse 17 teaches that Jesus is "at the center of the throne" and that He "will be [our] shepherd." He will lead us to springs of living water, and God will wipe away our every tear. Through our faith in Jesus and by His grace, heaven will be our eternal home!

Coming with the Clouds (Connect)

73. Perhaps one of the most underestimated assurances we have from the Bible is that our Savior is praying for us. If the prayers of a righteous person are powerful and effective (James 5:16), how powerful and effective are Jesus' prayers for us? The answer is self-evident, but we need to celebrate this reality more and more!

74. We can be filled with joy because we are saved, promised a gracious reward, comforted, consoled, and so on. The events of the Last Day will all be good for the child of God. All our sins are covered by the blood of Christ and remain that way for eternity! The reason for our confidence is the saving work of Christ for us through His life, crucifixion, and resurrection.

Our confidence is created and sustained by virtue of Christ's Word and Sacraments. In other words, we are confident not only because Christ has *won* our salvation but also because He continually distributes the benefits of this salvation through His Word and Sacraments. Both aspects are indispensable for our confidence and assurance. Having these, we are absolutely prepared for our Lord's second coming.

75. We Christians do not live in a foreign dualism that treats the body as inferior to the spirit. We honor our risen and coming Lord as we prepare ourselves in every way, including honoring Him with our bodies—the same ones that will be raised and enter the new heaven and earth.

Fully Prepared (Vision)

76. Answers will vary. Direct participants to the consistent blessings received through Word and Sacrament as God's people gather for worship. Note the mutual encouragement we share. (Check Hebrews 10:25.)

77. Responses will vary.

Appendix of Lutheran Teaching

Below you will find examples of how the first Lutherans described the person and work of Christ. They will help you understand the Lutheran difference.

The Augsburg Confession of 1530

Philip Melanchthon, a lay associate of Dr. Martin Luther, wrote the Augsburg Confession to clarify for Emperor Charles V just what Lutherans believed. Melanchthon summarized Lutheran teaching from the Bible and addressed the controversies of his day. This Confession remains a standard of Lutheran teaching.

Article III: Of the Son of God

Also they [our Churches] teach that the Word, that is, the Son of God, did assume the human nature in the womb of the blessed Virgin Mary, so that there are two natures, the divine and the human, inseparably conjoined in one Person, one Christ, true God and true man, who was born of the Virgin Mary. (*Triglotta*, p. 45)

Apology of the Augsburg Confession

Philip Melanchthon, a lay associate of Dr. Martin Luther, wrote the Apology to clarify for Emperor Charles V just what Lutherans believed. Melanchthon summarized Lutheran teaching from the Bible and addressed the controversies of his day. This Apology remains a standard of Lutheran teaching.

Article III. 261: Of Love and the Fulfilling of the Law

For Christ is a propitiation, as Paul, Rom. 3:25, says, through faith. When timid consciences are comforted by faith, and are convinced that our sins have been blotted out by the death of Christ, and that God has been reconciled to us on account of Christ's suffering, then, indeed, the suffering of Christ profits us. (*Triglotta*, p. 225)

Formula of Concord

Following Luther's death in 1546, confusion disrupted the Lutheran churches. Some wished to compromise on matters of doctrine in order to attain greater peace and unity with Calvinists and Roman Catholics. Others claimed to be true Lutherans but strayed from Luther's teaching. In 1576 Elector August of Saxony called a conference to clarify the issues. The result was the Formula of Concord (*concord* means "unity"), published in 1580.

Epitome IX. 4: Of the Descent of Christ to Hell

For it is sufficient that we know that Christ descended into hell, destroyed hell for all believers, and delivered them from the power of death and of the devil, from eternal condemnation and the jaws of hell. (*Triglotta,* p. 827)

Thorough Declaration III.15–16, 58: Of the Righteousness of Faith Before God

[Here is an elaboration on the connection between Christ's obedience (keeping and fulfilling the Law) and our being saved:]

For this reason, then, His obedience, not only in suffering and dying, but also in this, that He in our stead was voluntarily made under the Law, and fulfilled it by this obedience, is imputed to us for righteousness, so that, on account of this complete obedience, which He rendered His heavenly Father for us, by doing and suffering, in living and dying, God forgives our sins, regards us as godly and righteous, and eternally saves us.

. . . And faith thus regards the person of Christ as it was made under the Law for us, bore our sins, and in His going to the Father offered to His heavenly Father for us poor sinners His entire, complete obedience, from His holy birth even unto death, and has thereby covered all our disobedience which inheres in our nature, and its thoughts, words, and works, so that it is not imputed to us for condemnation, but is pardoned and forgiven out of pure grace, alone for Christ's sake. (*Triglotta,* pp. 919–21, 937)

Thorough Declaration VIII.6, 24, 40, 42, 44: Of the Person of Christ

(6) We believe, teach, and confess that the Son of God, although from eternity He has been a particular, distinct, entire divine person, and thus, with the Father and the Holy Ghost, true, essential, perfect God, nevertheless, in the fulness of time assumed also human nature into the unity of His person, not in such a way that there are now two persons or two Christs, but that Christ Jesus is now in one person at the same time true, eternal God, born of the Father from eternity, and a true man, born of the most blessed Virgin Mary, as it is written Romans 9:5: Of whom, as concerning the flesh, Christ came, who is over all, God blessed forever.

(24) . . . On account of this personal union and communion of the natures, Mary, the most blessed Virgin, bore not a mere man, but, as the angel [Gabriel] testifies, such a man as is truly the Son of the most high God . . . Therefore she is truly the mother of God.

(40) . . . For if I believe this [permit myself to be persuaded] that only the human nature has suffered for me, then Christ is to me a poor Savior, then He Himself indeed needs a Savior . . . (42) Now the person is true God; therefore it is rightly said: The Son of God suffers. For although the one part (to speak thus), namely, the divinity, does not suffer, yet the person, which is God, suffers in the other part, namely, in His humanity; for in truth God's Son has been crucified for us, that is, the person which is God . . . (44) so that it could be said: "God died," "God's passion," "God's blood," "God's death." For in His nature God cannot die; but now that God and man are united in one person, it is correctly called God's death, when the man dies who is one thing or one person with God. (*Triglotta*, pp. 1017, 1023, 1029, 1031)

Christological Controversies

Judaism (first century). Some early Jewish-Christian teachers regarded Jesus as truly a man and the Messiah. But they did not believe that He could also be truly God.

Docetism (late first century; named from the Greek word *dokeo*, "to seem or appear"). Influenced by Greek ideas about the corruption of the human body, Docetists taught that Jesus was truly God but only appeared to be human.

Adoptionism (second century). Some taught that Jesus was born an ordinary man but that God *adopted* Him as His Son at His Baptism.

Arianism (fourth century). Arius, an Alexandrian priest, taught that Jesus was truly a man and was also a god, created by the heavenly Father in the beginning. Arius's teaching greatly threatened early Christianity. After the struggle with Arianism, Christians agreed that Jesus was truly God and truly man. However, controversy began to emerge about how the human and divine natures related to each other.

Nestorianism (fifth century). Nestorius, a partriarch of Constantinople, sparked controversy by rejecting a traditional title for Mary, *Theotokos* ("God-bearer"; Mary bore the divine nature of Christ within her womb). Nestorius insisted on a new term, *Christotokos* ("Christ-bearer"). Opponents believed that Nestorius was reintroducing Adoptionist teaching. He was deposed. While in exile he wrote a defense before his death; it showed that his beliefs did not reintroduce Adoptionism. Most Syrian Christian churches were "Nestorian."

Eutychianism (fifth century). Eutyches opposed Nestorius and wanted to emphasize the divinity of Jesus. He taught that Jesus' human nature was like a mere drop of honey absorbed and lost in the ocean of His divine nature. His views were rejected because they did not correctly describe the human nature of Jesus.

Monophysitism (fifth century). The Council of Chalcedon (451) declared that Jesus had both a human nature and a divine nature. In reaction, a particular form of Eutychianism spread within Egypt and Palestine. This form held that the human and divine natures of Christ mixed with each other to produce one, unique nature. The modern Coptic church and Jacobite (Syrian) churches hold a Monophysite view.

Glossary

atonement. From an old French term for being "at one." Reconciliation between parties that were previously divided.

Christ. The Greek term for *Messiah*.

creed. From the Latin word *credo*, "I believe." Creeds are summary confessions of faith used by the vast majority of Christians. They developed at a time when most people could not read and needed a memorable rule of faith. See pp. 19–20.

Filioque. Literally, "and the Son." This Latin word was added to the Nicene Creed in the West to emphasize that the Holy Spirit proceeds from the Father *and the Son*.

Messiah. A Hebrew word meaning "anointed one,"—i.e., one chosen by God for a special purpose.

polemical. From the Greek word for "battle." The term describes conversation or writing that attacks and refutes.

propitiation. An act that appeases someone's anger. In the Scriptures the term describes the sprinkling of blood on the cover of the ark of the covenant on the Day of Atonement (Leviticus 16). The New Testament applies this term to the death of Christ.

reincarnation. A Hindu and Buddhist belief that people who die are born into another body and life, depending on how well they lived. Don't confuse this teaching with the Christian teaching about the *incarnation* of Jesus.

Son of God. A divine title meaning that Jesus shares the same nature or substance as the heavenly Father, just as a boy shares the same nature or substance as his father.

Son of Man. An Aramaic expression meaning simply "a person." The prophet Daniel made this a title for the Messiah (Daniel 7:13–14).

Theotokos. Greek for "God-bearer." A title for the virgin Mary, emphasizing that she gave birth to the Son of God, not just a typical human baby.